D0688143

BLAZERS™

MONSTERS

Vampires

by Jennifer M. Besel

Reading Consultant:
Barbara J. Fox
Reading Specialist
North Carolina State University

Content Consultant:
David D. Gilmore
Professor of Anthropology
Stony Brook University
State University of New York

★

Capstone

Mankato, Minnesota

Blazers is published by Capstone Press,
151 Good Counsel Drive, P.O. Box 669, Mankato, Minnesota 56002.
www.capstonepress.com

Library of Congress Cataloging-in-Publication Data
Besel, Jennifer M.
    Vampires / by Jennifer M. Besel.
    p. cm.—(Blazers. Monsters)
    Summary: "Describes the history and myths of vampires, their features, and
their place in popular culture"—Provided by publisher.
    Includes bibliographical references and index.
    ISBN-13: 978-0-7368-6443-5 (hardcover)
    ISBN-10: 0-7368-6443-1 (hardcover)
1. Vampires—Juvenile literature. I. Title. II. Series
BF1556.B47 2007
398'.45—dc22   2006000999

Editorial Credits
Aaron Sautter, editor; Juliette Peters, designer; Kelly Garvin, photo researcher/photo editor

Photo Credits
Bridgeman Art Library/Count Dracula, 1999 (oil on paper), Barry, Jonathan
    (Contemporary Artist)/Private Collection, 11; Count Dracula, illustration
    from the second issue of Boszorkany, 1890 (color litho), Kolonics, Istvan
    (fl. 1890)/Private Collection, Archives Charmet, 14
Capstone Press/Karon Dubke, cover, 4–5 (background), 6–7, 8, 9
Corbis/Bettman, 21, 26; John Springer Collection, 25; Michael & Patricia
    Fogden, 4–5 (foreground); zefa/Photex/Adrianna Williams, 20
Getty Images Inc./Hulton Archive, 16–17; Stone/Tim Flach, 12–13
Globe Photos/Supplied by 16x9, 27
Index Stock Imagery/Ewing Galloway, 28
Shutterstock/ChipPix, 16; Stasys Eidiejus, 18–19
Superstock/Lisette Le Bon, 22

The author dedicates this book to her husband, Jon, who protects her from
    all the monsters in the world.—J. B.

1 2 3 4 5 6 11 10 09 08 07 06

Table of Contents

A Midnight Snack

The moon casts an eerie glow on the old cemetery. Suddenly, a huge hairy bat appears. It soars away into the foggy night.

The bat lands outside a young woman's window. Its shape changes as it enters the room. It's no longer a bat—it's a vampire!

The vampire stands over the woman's sleeping body. The monster leans in for a meal of warm blood. Never satisfied, he leaves to find another victim.

9

Bloodsucking Monsters

People have told vampire stories for thousands of years. At first, vampires were part-animal and part-human creatures. But over time, vampires in stories became the make-believe bloodsuckers we know today.

BLAZER FACT

The most famous vampire story is about Count Dracula. Dracula was named after an evil ruler called Vlad Dracula.

Vampires are monsters that thirst for blood. They will drink animal blood if they have to. But they like human blood the best.

BLAZER FACT

Some stories say that if a vampire drinks all of a person's blood, that person becomes a vampire too.

13

14

In most stories, vampires are creepy and ugly. Vampires have very pale skin and sharp fangs. Their fingernails are long and yellow.

BLAZER FACT

A vampire's breath smells like rotting meat.

According to legend, sunlight kills vampires. During the day, vampires sleep in closed coffins. They only hunt for blood in the dark of night.

MORT DU CHOLERA

Vampires are dangerous shape-shifters. They fly through the night as bats. When they spot a victim, they turn back into vampires to attack.

BLAZER FACT

Vampires can also change into wolves or even clouds of mist.

Legends say that vampires hate garlic. They don't like crosses or holy water, either. These things can keep a vampire away. But they won't kill it.

It isn't easy to kill a vampire. In most stories, a wooden stake in the heart usually does the job. Bright sunlight or silver bullets can also kill vampires.

BLAZER FACT

Some stories say the only way to be sure a vampire is dead is to cut off its head.

Finding Vampires Today

Today, people often watch TV shows and movies about vampires. Usually, they are dark and scary. But sometimes the vampires are funny.

In the 1960s, *The Munsters* featured vampires as members of a strange, but funny TV family.

Most movie vampires are handsome men. They often wear tuxedoes and capes. They suck blood from the necks of beautiful women.

BLAZER FACT

Vampires in modern movies often have long hair and wear stylish clothes.

Every Halloween, people dress up to roam the night as vampires. We know vampires are not real. But it can be fun to scare our friends with vampire stories.

Glossary

cemetery (SEM-uh-ter-ee)—a place where dead people are buried

coffin (KAWF-in)—a long container into which a dead person is placed for burial

eerie (EER-ee)—strange and frightening

fang (FANG)—a long, pointed tooth

legend (LEJ-uhnd)—a story handed down from earlier times

shape-shifter (SHAYP-SHIFT-ur)—a person or thing that can change its shape or form at will

stake (STAYK)—a thick, pointed post

Read More

Knox, Barbara. *Castle Dracula: Romania's Vampire Home.* Castles, Palaces, and Tombs. New York: Bearport Publishing, 2005.

Miller, Raymond H. *Vampires.* Monsters. Farmington Hills, Mich.: KidHaven Press, 2005.

Oxlade, Chris. *The Mystery of Vampires and Werewolves.* Can Science Solve? Chicago: Heinemann, 2002.

Internet Sites

FactHound offers a safe, fun way to find Internet sites related to this book. All of the sites on FactHound have been researched by our staff.

Here's how:

1. Visit *www.facthound.com*

2. Choose your grade level.

3. Type in this book ID **0736864431** for age-appropriate sites. You may also browse subjects by clicking on letters, or by clicking on pictures and words.

4. Click on the **Fetch It** button.

FactHound will fetch the best sites for you!

Index